THE MOLD TRAGEDY
OF 1869

The Mold Tragedy of 1869

An Investigation

by

Jenny and Mike Griffiths

'The state is an instrument in the hands of the ruling class, used to break the resistance of the adversaries of that class.'

Vladimir Ilyich Lenin (1924)

ISBN: 0-86381-753-X

Cover design: Sian Parri

Illustrations on pages 33, 34 & top 35 were
kindly loaned by Ray Davies of Mold.
The remaining photographs were taken by Jenny Griffiths.

First published in 2001 by
Gwasg Carreg Gwalch, 12 Iard yr Orsaf, Llanrwst, Wales, LL26 0EH
☎ 01492 642031   🖺 01492 641502
✆ books@carreg-gwalch.co.uk   Website: www.carreg-gwalch.co.uk

DEDICATION

This book is dedicated to the memory of Mrs Hilda Evans, much loved Auntie of Earl Road, Mold, who sadly passed away before the book was completed. She supplied us with the family history and anecdotes which were so valuable, in particular history of our families connection with coal-mining at the Leeswood coalfield which was the centre of attraction in the 19th Century. We were told much about our distant relative Daniel Owen of Mold, much of which has never before come to light. Her enthusiasm will always be with us and always in our hearts.

ACKNOWLEDGEMENTS

The authors wish to thank Flintshire Archives Office at Hawarden for their help and assistance in researching this book, without their help it would have been impossible.

We thank our good friend Mr John Hughes Ll.B. Solicitor and Her Majesty's Coroner for north-east Wales for supplying historical facts. We are also grateful to York Railway Museum for their help with historical information concerning times of trains in 1869. The Meteorological Office at Bracknel, Berkshire for supplying information with regard to the weather for the summer of 1869 from their records.

We also thank the Cheshire Regiment at Chester Castle for supplying us with information regarding the military tactics used in the Mold Riot and for further historical information in the 19th Century concerning the control of rioters by the Military, and to Mr Peter Donnelly of The King's Own Royal Regiment Museum at Lancaster for the military history of Captain Blake who gave the fateful command at Mold during the riot.

We also thank Mr Ray Davies of Mold, photographer, who supplied us with historical photographs used in this book, and Mr John Roger Williams of Mold who searched the Parish Records so carefully and located the last resting place of Margaret Younghusband who was shot in the riot.

We also are most grateful to Dr Maurice Jones-Mortimer of Hertsheath Hall, Pontblyddyn, the High Sheriff of Flintshire for his assistance with the history concerning the village of Pontblyddyn and the coalfields in the 19th Century on his estate at Pontblyddyn, especially how the area was policed at that time.

We also thank John & Wendy Pickstock of Rossett, film-makers, who helped with the cover of this book with digital processing.

Finally, we thank Mr John Puw, our editor for the hard work he undertook in editing the manuscript and for his assistance with historical knowledge of life in the 19th Century.

If we have missed anyone out please accept our sincere thanks and our apologies.

CONTENTS

INTRODUCTION

Mold, Yr Wyddgrug, is the county town of Flintshire. It is an insignificant market town that comes alive when the farmers hold their market on Mondays and Fridays, or at least that is the impression it gives from its position nestling under the Clwydian range of hills.

The Romans probably came to Mold and built a small fort on the top of the Bailey Hill on High Street. No trace remains, however, since any construction of theirs disappeared when the Normans built a motte and bailey castle on the site in the 11th century. Such an abundance of forts might suggest a riotous history, and Mold did indeed become such a place. The disturbances were centred on the Leeswood and Coed-talon area collieries and it all culminated in the death of a number of people on June 2, 1869.

But what exactly were the reasons behind this bloody riot, and why were the soldiers so forceful? What caused a sleepy market town to become a battlefield where it was deemed necessary to use live ammunition? The story of the whole tragedy revolves around the small but highly productive coalfield of Leeswood Green Colliery in Leeswood village (Coed-llai) in the hills above Mold. The events went on to become known as 'The Mold Riot' or 'The Mold Tragedy of 1869'. This was not however a spur of the moment uprising for things had long been festering. And despite the bloody outcome, some good came of it in that it helped change the conditions under which colliers worked in the north Wales coalfields.

The authors were brought up in Mold and know this story well. Both our grandfathers and great-grandfathers were in the Leeswood collieries, and the older generation was present at the time of the riot. Mike Griffiths's great-grandfather is mentioned in the archive offices as being 'a hard man and over-seer'. His grandfather frequently spoke of his habit of going to Leeswood early in the morning and spending some time 'tickling' the local squire's trout in Afon Terrig. It was not that the trout were big and juicy, rather than being one that the colliers had over the landowner.

An amusing story concerns Jenny Griffiths's great-grandfather and grandfather. The elder of the two was a very gentle man and, apart from his work as a collier, was also a lay preacher in the chapel. The younger of the two was not so keen on religion and was fed up with being pestered about his non-appearance in the chapel on Sundays. It is obvious however that the young man thought hard on the matter. He took some fresh carrots from home and teased a donkey in a nearby field.

9

It being a Sunday, the faithful were in the chapel where they were joined by grandfather followed by a besotted donkey, while great-grandfather was in full flow in the pulpit. The congregation was amused by the appearance of this religiously significant beast of burden, but the elder of the two generations was not. The prank served its purpose however, since the hassle over the absences from chapel came to a halt.

Both authors have been fascinated by the story of the tragedy throughout our lives. We decided to delve deeper into the matter and came across some evidence that has never before appeared in print. We feel that the story is disappearing from the modern day Welsh culture of the area, and this is sad. It is a story of sacrifice that should not be forgotten, for it describes what was at best a most unfair business. Obviously, the events are well beyond living memory and we had to rely on a variety of archive materials in our research. What follows is the authentic presentation of those bloody events of a cool June day over one hundred and thirty years ago.

A BRIEF HISTORY OF THE
FLINTSHIRE COALFIELDS

Although it has long been the county town and market centre for the farmers of a wide area, Mold owes most of its wealth to mining and in particular to coal. The first recorded usage of coal in north Wales was by the Romans to melt metals at Fflint and also at Heronbridge near Chester. The coal is thought to have been mined at Ffrith near Wrexham and also at Halkyn. Coal was only mined on a small scale, usually by digging out what could be found near the surface. It was not until the Industrial Revolution of the 18th and 19th centuries that coal became king in its own right and the demands of industry became almost insatiable.

Prior to this, coal was mined in Wales on a local basis to heat great houses or for a limited trade with Ireland which had no coal deposits of its own. The larger pits in north Wales were in the coal rich areas of Mostyn and Wrexham. The whole industry was totally in private hands for most of the pits were sited on the big estates of the area. The size of the pit was largely governed by the wealth of the particular estate or on the amount of money that could be raised from shareholders, more often than not from other land-owning families over the border in England. Most coal continued to be extracted from shallow bell-pits. These were operated through lowering a collier in a bell shaped basket, the rate of descent controlled by a winch or sometimes a horse or ox. Coal was cut by hand and most pits realised a weekly output of about three tonnes. The bigger wealthier estates had deeper mines. Transportation was a severe problem as the roads were in a deplorable state with time being lost because of the damage caused to carts by the deep ruts in the tracks.

In 1709 Abraham Darby, a Shropshire man, discovered how gas could be extracted from coal thus leaving coke that could be used for smelting. The improvement this caused in the process of making iron made coal more and more important. This, as well as the improvement in road making that came about following the creation of Turnpike Trusts and the subsequent creation of the canal system, including the extension to Llangollen, meant that coal from Flintshire and Denbighshire could be sent to anywhere in the industrial belt of the Midlands and the North-West of England. Trade with Ireland also grew, and Welsh coal was exported there to keep the British troops who were stationed there warm.

The coal from the Treuddyn and Leeswood area of Flintshire was sent to the small ports on the Dee estuary following its canalisation in the 18th century, and from there it was exported to Ireland and the stations of the British empire around the world. Mining came to accompany farming as the major source of employment in Flintshire. Many colliers managed both occupations by mining through the winter months whilst wives and youngsters tended the animals, and then turning back to the land in high summer to harvest crops when coal was not so much in demand and many collieries closed down for the season. At the height of the industry, the Dee estuary had twenty-six ports to where coal was transported, prior to being exported by sea.

The colliers were mostly rural people who were trapped into a life of self-sufficiency or of poverty, or both. Mining was a tough and dangerous business and owners or shareholders rarely visited the pits, relying on reports from colliery managers and over-seers. Most of these people were constricted by a shoestring budget and miners' welfare was a dirty, unspoken expression. Most collieries were in English hands or under English financial control. Injuries were common, including fatalities, as were illnesses that were directly linked to the unhealthy way of life. Colliers received no benefits whatsoever. More or less their only option as a safeguard against their dangerous way of life was to pray against mishaps.

The big steam engines of Thomas Newcome were installed in the bigger collieries of Ewloe and Mostyn as early as 1712, when the amount of coal that could be cut was greatly increased. They were later introduced into the Flintshire lead-mines and were known locally as 'fire-engines'. Some of the equipment was made at Bersham near Wrexham. But despite the increase in the amount of coal that was being extracted, wages remained at as low a level as the owners could risk, and there was little change until the General Strike of 1926. Colliers, like everyone else, had to pay for medicine until the middle of the twentieth century, and this is one reason why they tended to have large families with the boys being sent out to work from an early age. Both Mike Griffiths's great-grandfather and grandfather were in full-time employment in the Flintshire coalfield by their twelfth birthday.

Women were also employed in the collieries, above and below ground. They washed coal, for the important families did not want their houses heated with dusty or muddy coal. They loaded wagons on site, and below ground they pulled trucks and also loaded the trucks, or 'pyches' as they were called. Children were 'employed' to open fire doors so as to allow free passage for ponies and trucks, or for the women pulling the trucks. Work started at 6.00am and a normal working day lasted for twelve to fourteen hours with Sundays off.

Records from Flintshire Archives for the Plas Teg colliery at Pontblyddyn, that was owned by the Trevor-Roper family, indicate the

12

wages for colliers and coal workers during the 17th century.

Coal Cleaners	6/-d per six days work
Labourers	9d per day
Women who were employed to carry water barrels	8d a day
'Pyche' pullers	8d a day

Plas Teg is now a private house on the A541 Mold-Wrexham road and is open to the public in the summer months. The coal spoil tips remain on the estate, and are always here to remind us how these resplendent houses came to be financed whilst the workers sweated and, in far too many cases, died young.

Wages in the local iron foundries were slightly higher but work was restricted to daylight hours and, in winter, production was accordingly low, as were the wages. Summer on the other hand gave an opportunity for some overtime. There are records of children of twelve earning 1/-d (one shilling = 5p) a day without overtime. Children were mostly educated, if they were very lucky, in Church schools at a cost of 2½d per week, but many worked.

The Earl of Shaftesbury urged Parliament to bring to an end the practise of employing children in collieries in 1842, and he cited the Flintshire coalfields as being especially bad. History records however that it was Flintshire that eventually brought about a change in the law making it an offence to employ anyone under thirteen years of age. The new Act of Parliament continued to be widely ignored by the owners of the bigger pits in the Ruabon area as well as in Flintshire. Records show that children as young as six or seven were employed above and below ground. Because of the social depravation of the time, single parents who had lost their partners and needed any income they could get just to keep the family alive also encouraged the practise.

The employment of young persons throughout the north Wales coalfield was under the control of Charter Masters who were hired by the landowners, but worked independently of them. Landowners were thus free of any liability when disaster struck. Most of the pits had English masters who were brought in to drive the Welsh harder in their work.

Many children were killed or seriously injured in the pits. They received horrific injuries to their hands and knees as they pulled the pyches loaded with 1½ to 2 hundredweight (about 75 – 100 Kg) of coal. Many children found that it was easier to push the truck with their heads, and this resulted in terrible neck injuries and even brain damage. The trauma caused to a child through being underground resulted in most pits having an under-age drinking problem. The Methodists were quick to seize on this particular problem and campaigned hard to stop it. Their case was that 'ponies were receiving better treatment than children, as children were easier to replace and cheaper than ponies'.

Mold was among the first towns to use coal-gas to light its streets and buildings. The Mold Cotton Factory on Denbigh Road (now Synthite Chemicals) was amongst the first in about 1812. Streets in Llangollen were lit from 1824 and in Wrexham from 1827. Street and factory lighting changed the lives of the people, but lighting underground remained a severe problem with the ever-present firedamp being easily ignited. Flintshire saw much protest from colliers' wives who objected to the wearing of a naked flame in leather helmet. Sir Humphry Davy's safety lamp of 1815 was a great improvement, and records show that the big colliery at Plas Isa, Acrefair near Wrexham was the first to use it.

Alongside the expansion of the collieries came the railway, with branch lines appearing across Flintshire from the main Chester to Holyhead line. As a result there was an increase in the pits in the Mold and Leeswood area, and a branch line opened from Mold to the Brymbo iron works. The people of Mold and the surrounding areas often used this line, and the authors rode it much as children and remember coal, minerals and livestock being moved along it.

The largest disruption to the coalfield was caused through absentee landlords and shareholders. They were mostly from England and rarely if ever visited the source of their great wealth, and had no contact whatsoever with the workmen who generated it. Local landowners used the press to advertise for investment in a proposed colliery or in the expansion of an already active colliery. Potential investors or shareholders did their business through their local banks or offices of commerce, and had no call to view the site of the investment, provided the returns on the investment were good and steady. Improving working conditions and workers rights would have adversely affected the financial figures in the short term, so very little was done without the workers applying an enormous amount of pressure.

When matters went wrong in the coalfield and the law had to intervene, the local landlords who owned the colliery and worried over their own investments, as well as their fellow shareholders, were more often than not the presiding magistrates. Since impartiality in law is a fairly recent concept, this did not hamper the magistrate's office in any way.

In our story, the main colliery is the Leeswood Green Colliery, which is now totally demolished. Archive records, however, clearly show why it was so important. A report from 1866 states that: 'the Leeswood seam is one of the richest in the area and possibly in north Wales to a depth of 95 yards, and this is below the main coal and it produces cannel which was discovered to the astonishment of every other colliery in the neighbourhood'.

Both paraffin and gas were extracted from cannel and prices at Leeswood Green rose to 28/-d (£1.40) per tonne for the best cannel. Smooth cannel fetched 9/-d (45p) per tonne. Curly cannel could produce as much as 90 gallons (410 litres) per tonne, smooth 30-35 gallons (136-158 litres) per tonne and some shales as much as 35 gallons (158 litres) per tonne. Although shale produced lighter and better oil, curly cannel was preferred for its greater productivity. Curly coal and cannel were smoother than the main coal, but harder than shale. Shale had a brown streak on it when scratched and the smooth cannel had a black streak. The main coal that was extracted from Leeswood, however, was a high quality hard steam coal that was used for shipping and railway engines.

A massive fault separates the Brymbo and Leeswood seams of coal, and also affects the Bromfield colliery at Mold. The fault is of limestone, making conditions very wet and dangerous for the colliers. But the main problem affecting the Coed-talon seam (Leeswood Green) was the porous nature of the bad cannel seams that allowed vast amounts of water to run through the workings from disused beds and lakes, trapped in the structure deep in the earth. Still, Leeswood Green produced some 7,000 tonnes of coal weekly at an average of 13/6d per tonne.

A look at a geological map of north Wales shows that the coalfields run from north Wales out through Cheshire into Lancashire, under both land and sea. Records from 1864 show that a staggering 93,000,000 tonne of coal was obtained across the United Kingdom, and that this coalfield yielded 2,000,000 tonnes of that total.

THE BACKGROUND TO THE DISTURBANCES

It has already been explained that absentee landlords from England largely financed most collieries with no contact between worker and owner. This caused understandable grievance within the mining community, and this was compounded by the owners and shareholders insistence on appointing senior management who came from English collieries, mainly from Durham. The owners wanted 'impartial' people managing the locals. They wanted people with whom they could communicate in their own language so that the desires of financial backers were passed on without hindrance.

Many of the local landowners were, originally, of Welsh stock but had spent their comfortable lives away in private schools or being educated abroad. This history goes back to the times of the Tudors when the Welsh nobility took the easy path to keeping their wealth and forsook their Welsh heritage. Many families added to their estates at the expense of less obsequious neighbours and others created vast new estates as a result of being granted lands for services rendered to further the causes of the English king of the period. Others forcibly took the land at the point of a lance, sword or musket because they knew that vast mineral wealth lay under the surface of the soil. Although many of the estates could trace their heritage back hundreds of years, the methods used by many owners to acquire their land was still of great public interest.

The colliers who worked under that land were particularly aware of this aristocratic history, and resented it strongly. They also resented the English Charter Masters and over-seers being promoted over local people. In many cases the Charter Masters were freelance and cared nothing for the colliers, be they Welsh or English. All they wanted was the best deal for themselves and a good relationship with their employer. They tended to be hard and unscrupulous men who bought and sold anything for hard cash. The owners accepted whatever they did as long as the profits kept coming in.

The colliers themselves, the ones doing the dirty, dangerous and all necessary work, could do nothing to affect the wishes of the owners or the masters. Records show that fights and riots were common occurrences in the areas of Wales under English masters, and death did result when the owners sought the assistance of the military to quell any uprising.

Colliers were paid by the ton of cut coal at the pit-head and when the seams ran low, the colliers were furious and worked like devils to cut through to the next productive seam. Waste was trucked to the surface but was not weighed so no one received any payment. At such times, the colliers probably worked harder than ever for themselves, but also for the owners, and got no recompense whatsoever for their efforts. Seams of waste affected all pockets of course, but it didn't cost the owners anything. Since the coal market was also governed by the weather and the Irish demand, any resulting pile-up of coal at the pit-head meant that it was the colliers who took the brunt by having their wages cut. The more fortunate men could then supplement their wages by working on the land and others, if they were near enough, worked in the numerous ports on the Dee estuary.

One documented problem was that many of the English over-seers actively disliked the Welsh and took every opportunity to place English colliers in the more fruitful seams whilst the locals often laboured in shale and rubbish in an attempt to get through to the next coal seam. This was a great source of resentment, but the masters invariably denied any involvement. The pit-head offices however kept accurate records of how much each collier earned and these figures were often quoted to supplement the Welsh colliers' argument.

Most of the Welsh colliers spoke only Welsh and very few of them were fluent in English. The over-seers and masters knew no Welsh and soon gained the common inferiority complex that comes of being aliens in a strange land where everybody speaks a different language. This is probably where the belief grew that everybody spoke in Welsh just to be able to discuss the bosses behind their backs. The Welsh colliers, in a tradition dating from Celtic times, also tended to pass all information from mouth to mouth and rarely wrote anything down. This is the biggest disadvantage possible for the modern historian since nearly all records are from the point of view of the over-seers, and documentation of what is an extraordinarily rich heritage is scarce by comparison.

The sight and sound of Welshmen communicating in their mother tongue in hushed voices underground concerned the masters. They claimed that the colliers might have been planning an insurrection. Since the masters did not understand a word, they were more or less powerless, and no Welshman would ever act as an informant. A decision was made that a strict 'No Welsh' policy be imposed. It is not known from where this rule originated, but the reasoning behind the rule was that a Welshman shouting a warning underground would not be understood by an Englishman unless the warning was in English. Managers had the ruling strictly imposed without considering the fact that there was now an even greater danger from a lack of communication, since the vast majority of the men underground knew no English.

The manager of Leeswood Green Colliery was John Young, a Durham man who, according to local legend, took great personal delight in imposing the 'No Welsh' rule at the colliery. Young was also more than a little benevolent to the English colliers at the pit, ensuring that they had a constant seam to work. Every local collier further disliked Young because he had replaced a rare species, for his predecessor at Leeswood Green Colliery had been a local manager. The unrecorded local man had been popular with the colliers, which might explain why he was replaced. Output certainly increased under Young and this was used to qualify the decision to replace the local man.

On May 17, 1869 Young placed a notice at the pit-head stating that the price of coal was to be cut during the forthcoming two weeks. This meant a cut in colliers' wages. In addition the Welsh colliers were already earning half of what they were used to since they had hit a nasty fault that caused water to flow into the pit. The Leeswood Cannel and Gas Company, an offshoot of the colliery, also informed its workers of a similar decision.

This was the last straw in a long running dispute between the hard pushed colliers and the owners of Leeswood Green Colliery. To make things worse, Young allegedly taunted the men, pushing them and their patience to the limits. When reports arrived at Leeswood Green about other Welsh collieries being affected, they decided to take action. It is alleged that on May 19, 1869, two days after the notices were posted, Young was assaulted by the colliers at Leeswood Green. He categorically denied any provocation on his part and went on to swear a complaint against several colliers, the matter to be heard before Mold Magistrates Court. Everything up to this point seemed to be fairly low-key and quiet but, when the hearing occurred, matters became crucial and all sense of reason was lost.

THE CASE FOR THE PROSECUTION

On Wednesday May 25, 1896, Ismael Jones, Edwin Jones, Robert Davies, John Jones, Richard Taylor, Thomas Jones and John Hughes appeared before Mold Magistrates Court. They had been arrested on warrant and were bailed to appear before the court a week later on June 2. All seven pleaded not guilty to the charges.

The Magistrates selected to hear the case were John Wynne-Eyton Esq., C B Trevor-Roper Esq., Edward Pemberton Esq., the Revd Jenkin-Davies, C Butler Clough Esq., Colonel Wills and Mr Henry Potts. All were local people and some had local mining interests and were landowners. A Mr Acton of Wrexham presented the case for the prosecution, and a Mr Swetenham from the company of Mr Sherrat, also of Wrexham, was instructed to appear on behalf of the defence.

The speed with which warrants were obtained was irregular with the normal police procedures of the time. The colliers were all in full-time employment, were all local, and all wanted to plead their innocence. The normal procedure would be to issue them with a summons to appear before the court. A warrant would only be applied should they fail to appear. The other reason for obtaining a warrant would have been that serious personal injury had been caused to the plaintiff, but this was not so in this case. The Wrexham Advertiser and the Chester Chronicle reported fully on the case that was heard at Mold Magistrates Court.

The prosecution put forward the case as follows. On the morning of May 19, 1869, Mr John Young left the colliery to take breakfast at his cottage nearby. He returned at about 9.30am to see a large number of colliers at the pit-head, all of them deep in discussion. Young sensed trouble and retired to the engine-house from where he could keep an eye on proceedings. Having watched the men for some forty-five minutes, he saw Noah Edwards approaching the engine-house. Young was aware that many of the men at the pit-head were from other collieries.

Noah Edwards asked Young to address the assembled colliers, who numbered over three hundred in Young's estimation. Young agreed on the condition that the men remained quiet and peaceful. Edwards said that this would be so and Young crossed the colliery to take up a position on a coal bank from where he attempted to explain the cut in coal prices and in the men's wages. Young said that the matter was beyond his control and that he, as a servant of the owners and shareholders, was doing nothing more than implementing their instructions.

Ismael Jones took several steps forward and asked Young to disregard the instructions on the grounds of immense hardship to the colliers.

Young claimed it was a management decision that was totally out of his hands, but that he was prepared to accompany the colliers with any complaint to the management or to the owners. He claimed that he was just a dedicated employee doing his job properly.

But the men had gone past the time for compromise and began moving towards him on the coal bank. There were shouts for his resignation and his departure from the colliery as soon as possible. The men informed Young of his unpopularity in the area and that he must leave quickly. Young protested that he, like them, was an employee and that the fault for the decision lay with the owners. All the bad blood and ill feeling of five years under Young however was quickly coming to the boil.

It was alleged that Ismael Jones moved forward and pushed Young to the ground. All attempts by Young to get back to his feet were thwarted by other colliers keeping him down. Young claimed in court that his working clothes were soaked from his being pushed to the ground, and this tallies with Meteorological Office records for the area that show that the night of May 18/19 saw heavy showers fading away at dawn. The pit-head would have been a mass of large dirty puddles.

When Young managed to regain his feet, he was again attacked. The men he accused were Robert Davies and Thomas Jones, who allegedly beat him around the neck until he again fell to the ground. Jones then kicked Young in the side. The prosecution stated that Robert Taylor was instrumental in the attack and that he enjoyed seeing Young lying in the wet and grime. The men were egged on by the shouts and encouragement of the other colliers who were also closing in around Young. He alleged that John Jones lost all sense of reasoning and seized a strong piece of wood of some 5 inches (13cm) in diameter. He raised it above his head so as to strike Young but the other colliers sensed that such a blow could result in a charge of murder and shouted at Jones to desist. It seemed an age before Jones took heed but the blow was not struck. Young, fearing the worst, lay still with his hands covering his head awaiting the blow. By now he was a terrified man indeed.

The violence and the potential for murder seemed to bring the colliers to their senses and Young seized his opportunity to get to his feet and made for the main gate. He unfortunately found that other colliers had locked it. The two men who restrained Young were William Hughes and Edwin Jones, the pursuing men having followed Young from the coal bank and shouted that he was not to be allowed out. The gatekeepers had no such intentions for there was much to discuss. The colliers had waited a long time to get Young into this position, running scared. They seized their moment and Young for his part pleaded for justice claiming that it was inhumane to treat him in this manner. But the colliers were long past listening.

It was stated in court that Young was held captive for some forty-five minutes, throughout which he claimed he was verbally abused in Welsh, which is a strange claim for a man who had no Welsh. It was a practise in those days to 'escort' offending managers, and even fellow colliers, from the colliery in a wheelbarrow or horse cart. They would be taken to the nearest railway station and sent on a one way ticket from the area. Coal was the most important commodity that the railways carried and coal was also their only fuel. It is not surprising therefore that the railways were sympathetic with the colliers and allowed free passage for any alleged offenders. There are many records of men being treated in this way in Flintshire during the late 19th century. Young complained bitterly to the court that, knowing his fate, he asked to be allowed home to change into clean, dry clothes at his home in Cae Gwiail, Leeswood. His request was not granted.

John Young told the court that there was no cart or wheelbarrow to hand on the day and that he was marched from the colliery to Leeswood, and then on to Pontblyddyn past the Bridge Inn. He was then taken to what is now the A5104 towards Penyffordd and on to the 'S' bends where there is a smithy on the left. Near the smithy is a marked footpath leading across fields to the former Hope Junction (Low Level) station or halt. The building is now demolished. It was here that the three hundred colliers handed Young over to PC McBride and PC Jones of Pontblyddyn police. PC Jones's day-book (see Appendix 1) records that he was at Hope Junction at mid-day on May 19, 1869, and the Railway Archives at York show that a train was due to depart towards Mold shortly after.

There is no mention in the officer's records of any fighting or ill treatment of Young on Hope station. Much speculation has been made as to why the officers were present at this time. It has been written that the officers had come to rescue Young from the clutches of the colliers, but PC Jones's records do not state this. What is far more likely is that the officers were simply waiting for the train to take them into Mold on routine business. The colliers' objective was probably to place Young on a train that, according to the Railway Archives, would be leaving in the opposite direction soon after. They wanted Young out of the country and Mold was only four miles away and still a dead end station in May, although an extension to Denbigh and on to the north Wales coast opened in September of the same year.

The sight of three hundred colliers frog-marching Young across the fields would have warned the constables that something was up, but it is probable that they were only there by coincidence. PC Jones had also visited Hertsheath Lodge on the same morning, presumably on the way to the station. Young was handed over to the two constables who escorted him to Mold. It was there that Superintendent Thomas took a written statement from Young about the assault.

On the following day, Superintendent Thomas and an unknown constable went to the Black Diamond Colliery in Coed-talon and there arrested William Hughes. Hughes accepted the police presence and accompanied them quietly.

The prosecution then went on to outline the events outside Mold Police Station in the Hall Fields in Mold. A crowd of three hundred gathered there to demand Hughes's release. The crowd was described as becoming 'ugly in its attitude towards the police...' Reverend Jenkins-Davies, the vicar of Mold, tried to quell the noise and objectors but to no avail. The police decided therefore to bring Hughes from his cell and the crowd moved in. Hughes was released and taken shoulder high through King Street, down Wrexham Street and out to Leeswood and on to Coed-talon. David Phillips saw him at the Black Diamond Colliery and attempted to persuade him to surrender to the police. Hughes eventually accepted that this would help matters, and the police released him on £60 bail to appear before Mold Magistrates Court. The police obviously accepted Hughes's version of events at this point.

When Young was called to the stand, he gave his personal details which stated that he had been a miner since 1831 and that he knew his job well. He explained to the court that an amount of coal had been surfaced that was mixed with shale and had not been sorted. He blamed this on the underground colliers and said that it affected the overall wages. He claimed that curly coal and smooth coal had come up mixed with shale in the same tub, and that it had not been separated, as it should have been.

Young went on to state that Ismael Jones had accused him of mixing the coals so that the colliers could be denied money. Young denied that this was so and then said that Ismael Jones told him bluntly 'You'll have to go for this'. Young then said that Jones turned to the colliers and said to them 'Lads, we'll see him off today for this'. There then followed a very heated exchange between Young and Ismael Jones and other colliers lasting over half an hour.

Young then detailed the assault upon him by the colliers and he alleged that he was thrown into an empty coal tub. He gave details of his abduction from the colliery and his march to Hope Junction. He was precise and exact in his evidence.

It was alleged that Young had an aggressive attitude towards the colliers and that Welsh colliers had been purposefully placed on poorer seams to ensure that they earned smaller wages, He denied this strongly. It was then alleged that he had known that there was a shortage of pit props underground and that he had again purposefully obstructed the colliers by not ensuring that they had proper supplies. It was the practise in some collieries to do this to keep wages down. The shortage of pit props continued until after World War 1 when the shortage in the trenches had forced measures to address the problem. The Forestry Commission was formed to ensure that pit props would never be in short supply again.

Young denied that he himself had ever created a shortage of props and placed the blame for the problems on supplies, saying that he could not send down what was not at the pit-head. Where a shortage of props had arisen, it was the practise to leave uncut verticals of coal to act as natural props. Uncut coal did not weigh anything and would not count in collier's wages. This was again a common practise with some of the managers.

Young told the court that Ismael Jones had never complained to him about working on a face through which water was pouring. His complaint had been about the water itself. Young categorically denied that he was supposed to have told colliers that they need not worry about poor seams or water, since there was much worse to come. The colliers present in court arose *en-masse* in uproar claiming that Young was lying.

Evidence was then given regarding colliers' wages and exactly how the money was distributed. Welsh colliers earned a top rate of 4/6d (26p) a day compared to the English miners maximum of 7/6d (37p) per day. The Welsh colliers claimed that whilst they worked in gangs of six or seven, the English were given better faces and were consistently placed in the more lucrative parts where there was a better chance of earning a living. All the colliers wanted to cut cannel, in itself a term from the north-east of England, because it was the better earner.

William Hughes, one of the defendants was married to an Irish girl. Young was alleged to have called her a Fenian, an allegation that he strongly denied. He also denied having an abusive attitude towards Mrs Hughes because she was Irish. The allegations regarding Young's relationship with the Hughes's went on to state that, when Mrs Hughes approached Young about the cut in her husband's wages, Young subsequently placed her husband on a poor vein from which there was little hope of cutting much coal. Young denied everything saying that the

English colliers were known as 'fancy-men' or 'toadies'. He went on to deny any favouritism towards the English colliers at the expense of the local men.

William Boukley was called to give evidence, presumably being one of the 'fancy-men'. He presented the court with exacting evidence of the attack upon Young, that he had witnessed, including his telling the court that he had seen Young being pushed into an empty coal-tub. He said that he had been at the colliery for eighteen months and was at a loss as to why there was so much hostility towards John Young. He denied that he was a 'toadie', or that he constantly received favourable treatment from Young. He went on to deny that the English colliers were receiving more money for their work than the Welsh, but couldn't explain the ledgers that clearly supported the Welsh colliers' claims. Several other colliers were called to give evidence, presumably all Englishmen since their evidence is all fairly stereotyped and supports Boukley's version of events.

Alexander Ward was then bought to the stand. He was the resident secretary in the Leeswood Green Colliery and produced ledgers from the colliery office. The ledgers clearly showed that the English were taking home more than the local men. While the average wage in 1869 was 4/1½d (20p) per day for a twelve-hour shift, Ismael Jones realised only 2/9d (13p) per day. Ward had a simple explanation when questioned about this. He said that the English were better colliers and worked harder. They spent less time standing about talking. There were one hundred and thirty-two colliers at Leeswood Green, of who only seven were English. Whether Ward himself was English or Welsh is not recorded.

The evidence of Alexander Ward brought the prosecution's case to a close. When outlining the case to the bench, the prosecution made no attempt to hide the fact that they considered a custodial sentence to be the only viable option should a conviction be returned. The defence was still to make its case.

THE CASE FOR THE DEFENCE

Mr Swetenham opened his case with a bullish attack on the arrest of his clients by warrant. He desired to know of the court why warrants were issued outright when it was the usual practise to issue summonses. The clerk of the court, Mr Roper, replied that it was usual practise for warrants to be issued upon information being laid on Oath.

The courtroom, packed to the door, was silent as Mr Swetenham went on at some length. He said that the case was of the gravest concern to everyone, and reiterated his own concern over the issue of warrants instead of the usual summonses. He felt that a heavy-handed approach had been deployed from the outset, especially since the defendants were most anxious to conclude proceedings and that it was never their intention to thwart the issue of summonses. He said that all the defendants had total faith in the magistrates living amongst them who were not themselves employers of labour, because their interest was to stand between defendant and employer.

Mr Swetenham deplored violence and the fact that violence had been used. He said however that the colliers had no avenue of appeal other than through John Young, the underground manager. He then said: 'Had not John Young made himself obnoxious to others and to several men in Leeswood Green colliery? And was not the presence of so many other colliers from neighbouring collieries... in support a matter that trumpeted the fact that Young had not only aroused his own workmen, but those of surrounding collieries to manifest their opinion of him...

Suppose the six or seven Englishmen were put in good places by Young; to whom shall the Welshmen complain in lieu of there being no director there? They had to complain to Young... I am shaken to hear that the prosecution in this matter claims that a fine is insufficient... The prosecution are in fact making scapegoats of the defendants for the assembled three hundred men at the colliery on that date.

If the outcome of this case is important to the company, then it is tenfold more important to the men concerned... I must ask the bench to put themselves in the position of these men earning a living by being a collier and all the uncertainties of that job, and whether they were prepared to go underground and make such complaints to a manager like Young after a drop in wages?

Young was put there as a go-between for the directors and the men, to see that the men had proper pay and that the directors were informed of the movement in the price of coal.'

Swetenham then turned to the events. He alleged to the court that

Young had simply fallen on the empty coal tub, and that there was no direct evidence to show otherwise, as there was no direct evidence to say whom, if anyone, had pushed Young. Young alleged that Thomas Jones had kicked him – yet, said the defence, he wasn't even at that location at that time. He went on to assert that the prosecution had failed to offer evidence as to whom had kicked Young and that it was therefore open to the bench to acquit the men on that charge. Swetenham protested to the court that there was no evidence against William Hughes and Edwin Jones, other than their having prevented Young from leaving the site. This could not be anything more than a technical assault, protested Mr Swetenham. Robert Davies and Thomas Jones were also innocent because Young had fallen on the coal tub. The truth was that there was such a disturbance on the colliery site that day that nobody really knew what was going on.

The matter of Young falling on the coal tub was nothing more than general pushing and shoving between Young and the men. It was for the bench to decide the extent of assault, if there was any. Much of Young's evidence was uncorroborated, but the facts were most important to the whole county. 'Every day when capital comes into play like this, we are more likely to see more and more matters like these.'

Mr Swetenham then called John Roberts to the stand. Roberts agreed that Ismael Jones had been there but denied that he was the spokesman for the men. He had asked Young about the wages on behalf of the men and that was all. Young had insisted that some of the colliers earned as much as 5/6d per day, and Ismael Jones had claimed that the high earners were all 'fancy-men'. Roberts went on to tell the court that there had been some pushing and shoving among the men, but that it was the crowd moving that had caused Young to go down, and not a living man could say who had done what that day. He said that he had not seen John Jones strike Young and that the latter fell over the tub unaided.

'The men were like a lot of geese eating', he told the court. 'They were popping in and out all over the place. You couldn't see who was who, or what was what!'

He told the court that he personally had complained to Young about the lack of pit props. All the men had complained on this point for a period of six weeks, but no new supplies had been forthcoming.

Thomas Williams swore an oath that he earned between 1/11d (9p) and 3/6d (32p) per day. He was present on the day in question but it was impossible to say what happened and he doubted that anyone else could state what had happened with any clarity. Richard Roberts said that he had been in a position to view most of the proceedings and that he had not seen anyone strike Young. If it had happened as Young claimed, then he could not have helped but see it. John Evans told the court under oath that he had been with the prisoner Thomas Jones. He gave evidence of Alibi but could not give evidence of the time factor to support it when pressurised by the prosecution. Mr Acton submitted with success that Evans's evidence of Alibi could not therefore stand.

Mrs Elizabeth Hughes then came to the stand and gave evidence that she had approached Young regarding her husband's wages. Young, she alleged, had been offensive to her, promising that the men would eat peelings before very long. He had then attacked her for being Irish and a Fenian. Mrs Hughes's evidence concluded the case for the defence. Final submissions were made on behalf of both the defence and prosecution and the Magistrates retired to consider their verdict.

No evidence was given at any time regarding any injury to John Young. Should he have been pushed to the extent that he claimed, and also kicked by angry, physically strong men wearing leather boots, then it would be supposed that there would be damage of some kind to offer as evidence in support of his claims. He was taken to Mold and interviewed by Superintendent Thomas soon after the affray and any physical injury would have been mentioned in the subsequent report. No such evidence was offered. The only substantiated claim that he made was that he had a wet and dirty suit of working clothes. The policemen who took him from the colliers at Hope Junction reported no more than this. Should he have been injured, or should there be any blood or bruising showing, then it might be supposed that one or other of the two officers would have mentioned it in his day-report.

In legal terminology, the assault on Young would be rated no higher than a case of common assault – a complaint that police stations receive daily. The usual response to such a complaint is for the plaintiff to seek a solicitor since the police can only take action if visible injury has occurred. Young even seems to have accepted that he was in the wrong since he asked at the colliery gate to be allowed home to change into clean, dry clothes. He knew the way of the Flintshire collieries well enough and, once the gates were open, there would be no return for him.

The greatest truth told to the court was probably by John Roberts. There was such a melee at the colliery on that morning that no one could be certain as to what happened. There was certainly pushing and shoving going on, but much of it would have been collier on collier with a very frightened colliery manager confronting the mob. There was a distinct lack of evidence upon which to convict any man, whereas concrete evidence such as that of the colliery ledger was hardly touched, and was deemed too insignificant to be the cause of the disturbance.

THE COURT'S VERDICT

The Magistrates returned after a brief period of retirement. Mr Trevor-Roper, the chairman, announced a finding of guilt on all counts. He went on to inform the defendants of their sentences, starting with Ismael Jones and John Jones.

'It appears that you two are guilty of the most severe of offences. You are the ringleaders. We have decided that you shall be gaoled for one month each with hard labour.'

The courtroom, which had until this point been in a state of dignified silence, suddenly erupted in chaos with people shouting and surging forward with arms waving. Trevor-Roper was unperturbed and turned to address William Jones and Edwin Jones.

'It appears that neither of you struck John Young and therefore we fine you 10/-d (50p)'. This was a week and half of wages, which could mean a week in gaol in lieu of the fine. Trevor-Roper then addressed Robert Davies, Richard Taylor, Thomas Jones and John Hughes, the remaining defendants. He bellowed;

'You all committed an assault upon John Young and are therefore fined £1 each with costs, or fourteen days in gaol with hard labour.

There seems to have been considerable hostility towards Young but really, after the evidence we have heard there seems no need of it. We hear he said this or that, but there is no evidence to show so.

It does not appear that the Englishmen were favoured and therefore you should have had no aggression towards them. We hope this is a warning to you all and that you never take the law into your own hands again because the Magistrates have the power to punish you, if you do so. I recommend that you go home peacefully.'

There then followed a discussion as to whether the court should deal with a further charge that had been made. It concerned colliers breaking into John Young's home and removing his furniture onto a cart on which it was conveyed to the railway station. The information suggested that Mrs Young, who was in the property at the time, had also received a minor assault from the colliers. The railway company subsequently held the furniture until after the case was heard, when the court made arrangements for its release.

Mr Acton for the prosecution was ready to lay the charge before the court but Mr Swetenham had other ideas. There was considerable relief when the terrified John Young saw sense and agreed with the defence that the charge be withdrawn. Trevor-Roper had to have his say however and, leaning across, shouted to the prisoners; 'It is wrong to break into a man's house and remove his furniture. Had the case stood, the punishment would have been a lot harsher than the assault case.' The outburst brought proceedings to a close.

It seems almost unbelievable that the above was all heard within the span of six short hours. A contested case such as this today would have run for a week, and would have appeared before a jury rather than a magistrate's court. It is clear that certain parties were in a rush to bring matters to a head and at the same time establish a point. Trevor-Roper even implied that the further charge that was not brought before the court would have been found guilty regardless of the fact that not a scrap of evidence had been heard. It is also clear that the evidence regarding Young's treatment of the colliers, and his contempt for Mrs Elizabeth Hughes being Irish, went totally unnoticed by the bench since Trevor-Roper commented that they could not see why Young was so disliked.

What is more, there is much reference to assault, but not a scrap of evidence or even mention of the fact that Young received any physical injury or damage. Where concrete evidence was offered regarding the relative earnings of the Welsh colliers compared to the English colliers at the pit, the court chose to totally ignore it.

THE RIOT

The area of the County Hall, known as the Hall Fields, was very different to what can be seen today. The outline of the Hall Fields remains a stone wall sloping down to what was the railway line (now an access to a supermarket car park). Below this stone wall was an embankment descending to the railway that in the years following the Second World War served as a long market garden, run by Italians who decided to stay at the end of the war. The entire area from the wall, through where the cattle market now stands, was then a grassy field with trees growing on it. The fields extended to the rear of property on both High Street and Chester Street. There were two smithy's, one in King Street around where the Black Lion once stood, and the other to the rear of where the Grosvenor Arms stood at the junction of High Street and Chester Street.

The County Hall was then a barracks with the police station and lock-ups being situated at the King Street end of the block. It was erected in 1858 and is clearly outlined on the 1871 council map. Prior to this incident in 1869, the barracks had been strengthened for fear of attacks from local colliers, such incidences being common in the area, and from Irish nationalists who were known as Fenians. There had been Irish trouble in the Flintshire coalmines for some time. Ireland was in the grips of famine and many men came to work in the coalmines, and did so for food in lieu of wages. This caused resentment amongst the local colliers and the barrows and carts were in constant use. The coalmine owners, however, were glad to employ Irish workers. For one thing, they were willing to work for no more than a slave would get for his labours. But almost as importantly, the owners felt that, in doing so, they were protecting themselves against attack from Irish nationalists. The building remained under the control of the War Office until 1878 when it was leased to the council. It was demolished in the 1970s. Grosvenor Street did not exist in 1869, and Lower Chester Street was only then under construction. The railway bridge had been built in 1866. Chester Street, in those days, turned right into Grassy Lane or Tyddyn Street, as it is now known. The town's first fire station was built in Ponterwyl and the horses for drawing the engines grazed outside the Hall Field Buildings or County Hall. The area where the Victoria Inn stands, and to its rear where there is an auction room and houses, was a huge gravel quarry in 1869 from where material was obtained to build Chester Street. Stones had been piled at the quarry entrance. The whole area was roughly cobbled and the approach road to Mold Railway Station and Telegraph Office was rough and covered in potholes and stones. There was enough ammunition there to start a small war.

The crowd was in a state of high alert as people left the court onto the Hall Fields. One collier called Phillips, probably David Phillips of Coedtalon, appealed for peace but his attempts to address the crowd was shouted down despite his support for the colliers. The women in the crowd vowed that they would not leave without their men, and that no one would go to gaol. Tension was at breaking point as the crowd moved in the direction of the gates on Hall Fields and Chester Street.

Flintshire had occasion to form a constabulary during the 1860s, and the first incumbent of the post of Chief Constable was a Mr Peter Browne. He received a salary of £225 and was provided with a horse for his travelling needs, as well as keep for the animal. He was apparently a man who was '...small in stature with a very loud voice and a good sense of discipline'.

Browne was aware of the danger on this day since he had experienced colliers rioting in the past. He therefore took extensive precautions in his preparations for June 2, 1869, calling all the men under his command from as far afield as Bangor-on-Dee (Bangor Is-coed). He had also telegraphed Chester for assistance in the morning and soldiers from Chester, who arrived on the 10.00am train from Chester, were already billeted in the town centre barracks whilst the officers were in the greater comfort of the Black Lion Inn. Flintshire Yeomanry had been detailed to protect vulnerable buildings, such as the town's armoury where firearms and ammunition were kept.

Throughout the day he had watched men, women and children streaming into Mold and converging on the County Hall. Although the Chief Constable was not a legally minded man, his military background and planning were of greater use in this situation. And even with the withdrawal of the charges against those who entered Young's house, his previous experience in the town led him to expect trouble.

By 6.00pm, Tyddyn Street was heaving with a crowd estimated at about two thousand strong. The Railway Bridge had been manned by colliers, as was the station approach. It was obvious that the crowd was planning mischief, the women especially. By 7.00pm the estimated crowd had grown to as many as three thousand. A number of men had been seen crossing the Hall Fields towards King Street and the turnpike road to Fflint. It was assumed that they would lie in wait there in case a horse drawn prison-van should pass taking the prisoners to Fflint Castle (the then notorious county gaol). Browne had spotted the potential for disaster along this route and chose to use the normal train service as a means of transporting the two prisoners to Fflint. He only had to move

Railway Station, Mold – scene of the riot June 2nd, 1869

Wrexham Street, Mold. Date of photo uncertain but estimated to have been taken around the time of the riot. This is how Wrexham Street looked when the colliers marched into Mold on the 2nd June, 1869, and the injured were carried along this street to Pontblyddyn.

The County Hall, Hallfields, Mold. This is the building where the colliers were tried. The extreme right of the photo was the armoury where the militia were based.

High Street, Mold as it looked at the time of the Mold Riot.

The Goal, Mold. The actual goal itself was situated to the rear of this imposing building. It was here the colliers were transferred from Fflint Castle (goal). The building later became a College and is now a private residence.

The Bridge Inn, Pontblyddyn. Relevant to the Mold Riot story. It was here the colliers were given their free ale.

The Boars Head Inn, Mold (Chester Street). It was here that the inquest on those killed in the Mold Riots (2nd June 1869) was held. The property has not changed structurally since the time of the riot.

This wall in Tyddyn Street, Mold was the same one mentioned in the Riot 1869 from where the colliers and their wives were alleged to have stoned the police and army escort as they made their way down the (then) station approach.

This is the 'Free Church' Tyddyn Street, Mold which is mentioned.
The original tower has since been demolished.

Margaret Younghusband, who was shot in the riot, is buried at the back of Mold Parish
Church. We are unable to trace the exact location of her grave. Proof of her burial is in the
Church Parish Records. This photograph was taken prior to the alterations in 1957.

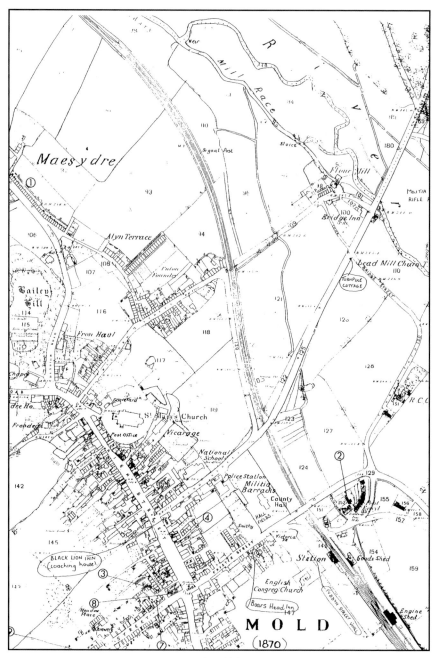

Map of Mold (1870)

38

This is the only known copy of the Mold Riot at 1869. The artist is unknown but this print appeared in the Press shortly after the Riot. Although a generalisation of the scene is wholly inaccurate and appears to have been drawn by someone outside the Mold area.

THE
Coleshill Colliery Co.

BEG LEAVE TO ACQUAINT THE
INHABITANTS OF

HOLYWELL AND GREENFIELD,

THAT THEY MAY BE SUPPLIED WITH

GOOD
COAL

At Five-pence $\frac{1}{2}$ per cwt.

AND THE VERY

BEST MAIN COAL

Excelled by none for House use,

At Seven-pence per cwt.

Delivered at their respective Dwellings.

All Orders sent to the Clerk at the Colliery, will be punctually attended to.

Coleshill Coal Works,
    May 21, 1823.

CARNES, PRINTER, HOLYWELL.

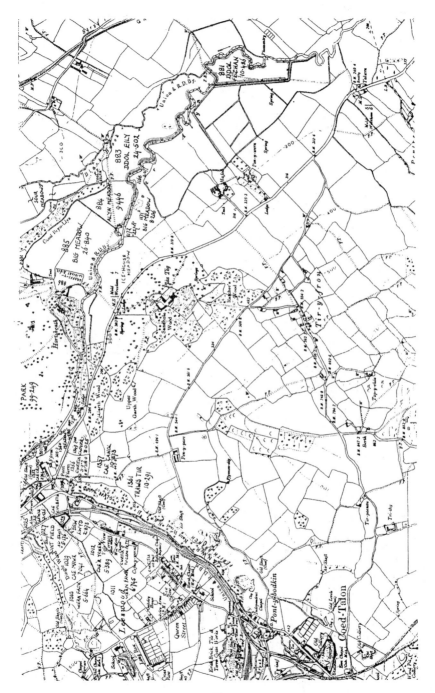

41

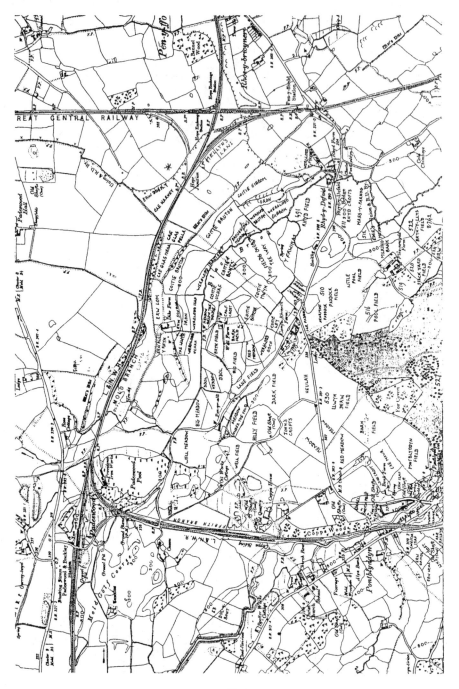

two chained men from the Hall Fields to the station, a distance of no more than 200 yards (190 metres). The area, however, was littered with ammunition that would be deadly in the hands of an angry crowd.

A runner was dispatched to hold the 7.15pm train to Chester at all costs until the two prisoners were on board. Shrewd move as this might have seemed, but the view of the 200 yards from the County Hall to the railway station must have looked more like 200 miles. The train, however, chugged into the station on time and Browne was informed that it would await his instructions.

The order was given to open the gates to allow the prisoners and their escort out. The crowd reacted angrily and it took some time for the gates to open against the pressure of people doing their utmost to keep them closed. During the long delay, the first stone was thrown that struck one of the escort. Inspector Hughes of Mold and PC Lockwood of Bangor-on-Dee moved to secure the shackled prisoners as the volley of stones grew in intensity. With blood streaming, they tried to push their way towards the railway station. Inspector Hughes was struck on the head and nearly lost his senses but the escort somehow managed to keep moving forward under a constant hail of stone and rocks. Many of the men throwing the rocks, which were carried by women from the Tyddyn Street quarry, were undoubtedly heightened in their violence by drink.

The imperative was to get the escort and prisoners down the slope and through the iron gates to the relative safety of the Chester platform on the far side as soon as possible. Some of the officers were recorded to be carrying cutlasses but no mention is made that they were drawn at any time. Browne still knew that the task would not be easy with the barrage of missiles raining down and the endless abuse that was aimed at the officers in both Welsh and English.

The Chief Constable's worst fears however were becoming a reality as men and women in the crowd had been caught in the hail of stones from the elevation of Tyddyn Street. Much was made in subsequent reports of pieces of masonry weighing some 4-5 pounds being collected as evidence. These could not have been thrown from Tyddyn Street since it was too far, and large pieces thrown from such a height would have undoubtedly caused serious or even fatal injuries. It is clear from studying the area that these would have been thrown by persons close to the escort.

The escort and prisoners continued their inch by inch shuffle down towards the station building. A major problem had developed since the railway station staff had closed the gates, probably due to losing their nerve. The worst injuries inflicted upon the escort occurred during the ten minutes that they spent begging to be allowed through. At last, a small door was opened through which the escort and prisoners hurried onto the platform. At this point they came under the canopy of the station, which afforded them shelter from the stoning if not the abuse. The railway staff again appears to have taken fright, however, and threw open the large metal gates through which carts came to unload and to load from the train. The crowd surged forward again and hundreds fell onto the platform. The barrage re-started as the escort and the prisoners crossed to the still waiting train, which itself became the target of the stone throwers. Several windows were damaged and it is easy to imagine the engineer and fireman pulling the whistle, demanding to get away. The signal was long off and it was time they were away since connections had to be made in Chester. But the hail of missiles was too intense for the train to move. Chief Constable Browne was getting more and more afraid that loss of life would occur and sought Captain Blake, whom he found nursing a badly injured head. Browne begged that the soldiers be ordered to fire above the crowd in an attempt to bring them to their senses. Blake however was adamant that this could not happen since the Riot Act had not been read, and he needed a magistrate's permission to do so.

Browne then desperately sought a magistrate in the crowd. He might have seen the magistrates, who had previously presided with such dignity, at the top of the station approach, but there was definitely no passage for them to the station. After some time, a frightened train passenger called Mr Clough from Chester, whom it was claimed was a magistrate, came forward and instructed Browne to give Blake the right to order his men to open fire. Blake was again unsure of the legal position in respect of the failure to read the Riot Act, and it was only with considerable reluctance that he gave his men the order to open fire.

The Riot Act at the time was a long drawn out speech that had to be read aloud to the assembled rioters. It warned them that if they did not desist from rioting, then the police could take whatever action they deemed necessary to stop the action. In practise, by the time the speech was over, the rioters had often calmed down and the riot had in all probability ceased. It was not read out on this June evening in Mold.

The crowd was by now attempting to uproot the iron fencing on the railway station boundary. It was at this moment that the crack of a rifle volley sounded but the crowd was too far gone to take any heed and did not realise the seriousness of the situation. Browne realised that firing over their heads was little more than a waste time and, following further consultation with Captain Blake, the order was given to fire into the body of the crowd.

Aim was taken and another controlled volley this time had the desired result, as well as the direst of consequences. Edward Bellis, a young blacksmith from Treuddyn, fell to the ground holding his stomach. Friends grabbed his reeling body and took him away by horse and cart from Chester Street to Pontblyddyn. The door of the Druid Inn was slammed in their faces and they continued to another public house lower down the village. The young man died in the Queens Arms (now demolished) in the arms of his friends at 1.00am the following morning.

Robert Hanaby was a nineteen-year-old collier from the Black Diamond Colliery in Coed-talon. He was standing on Tyddyn Street from where he was throwing stones and was obviously singled out as a target by a soldier. He was shot in the face and was dead before he hit the ground. Mrs Elizabeth Jones had been supplying stones to the ones who were throwing. It was also alleged that she herself had been hurling stones at the escort. She was shot in the back and eyewitnesses said that the bullet emerged through her breast. Friends took her to a cottage in Chester Street where she died some days later.

Margaret Younghusband was simply in the wrong place at the wrong time. She was a nineteen-year-old orphan from Chester who had only arrived in Mold that morning to take up a position as a housemaid at a large property on the High Street. She had gone with friends to clean the Presbyterian Chapel (Capel Mawr) in New Street, where her employer was the minister, and had followed the crowd in the direction of Chester Street. She was no more than a casual observer caught up in the melee, and was merely standing in the crowd watching the proceedings when she suddenly fell clutching her thigh. The damage was so severe that, despite being taken to Dr Williams's surgery on the High Street, she quickly died from loss of blood. Her aunt lived in Garden Place in Mold (now demolished) and it is known that this lady arranged for the girl's burial.

Christopher Keane was the highly respected manager of the Mold Iron Foundry and was a recognised dignitary in the area. He was walking in Tyddyn Street, strange as this may seem, and was another innocent bystander who became a victim. He was shot through the shoulder but was more fortunate than the others since records suggest that he made a painful, but full, recovery.

Five stone throwers were arrested by the military but none of their details are recorded. There were also stories, some taller than others, of lucky escapes. One unrecorded lad was shot through the ear whilst another lost part of a finger to a stray bullet. Bullets lodged in the walls all over the area and were proudly dug out as souvenirs. Stories of those that were missed by inches abounded. The official figure was that twenty people were injured by bullets and survived, but the exact figure will never be known. Many received first aid and treatment in the nearby pubs and houses, but many ran away with their injuries for fear of being arrested by the police for stone throwing.

The riot stopped when people began falling and the crowd soon dispersed. Chief Constable Browne directed that the prisoners be held in Chester Castle (Gaol) that night before being transferred to Fflint Castle (Gaol) the following day. Ironically, it is known that Fflint Castle ceased to serve as a gaol around this time and that all the prisoners were sent to Mold gaol. It is not known whether Ismael Jones and John Jones served their time in Fflint, or whether they were moved to Mold.

The soldiers who had fired the volleys left Mold on the 10.00pm train, the last of the day to Chester. They were replaced by one hundred and eight men from Chester under a Major Patten. Captain Cottingham and Lieutenant Dean were given the responsibility of guarding the town's armoury for that night.

The streets were deserted on the day after the riot, although small groups of people gathered to discuss the events of the previous day. Browne had asked all his men, including those who were injured if possible, to report for duty as a show of strength and defiance to the colliers in the area. Many officers accepted the challenge and reported for duty with their heads bandaged and many in great pain. Estimates were made for the damage that was caused by the riot and attempts were made to bring the town back to normality. Soldiers assisted the police with their patrolling duties but there were no reports of any further hostilities towards either the police or the troops.

THE INQUEST

The weather in Mold on the day of the riot was very much as it had been on the day of the disturbance. By the beginning of the inquest on June 4, 1869, Mold was again bathed in bright sunshine and good order was restored. The inquest was held at the Boar's Head Inn, Chester Street and was opened by Her Majesty's Coroner, Peter Parry Esq. of Mold. The members of the jury were William Jannion Jones (foreman), William Jones (ironmonger), B Powell (confectioner), Humphrey Lewis (grocer), John Edwards (draper), William Davies of Cambrian House, J Halcroft, Evan Jones (currier) John Davies (painter), John Price (currier), Job Edwards (confectioner), John Evans (grocer), J P Kennain of the Crown Vaults, Edwin Pownall (grocer) and John Evans (grocer).

The jury was sworn in and taken to view the bodies, including going to Pontblyddyn to view the body of Edward Bellis. This was the custom in those days, and the body was frequently displayed in the room where the inquest was conducted. Perhaps that this time they overlooked the custom since there were too many bodies to accommodate. There followed a discussion as to whether the inquest should then be adjourned for the day. Some jurymen however felt it better to press on with the matter since there was considerable discontent in the area about the fact that the army had fired without first reading the Riot Act. In fact, the Riot Act had not been read at all in this case, and the jury felt that this caused considerable concern.

The coroner however weighed into the jury claiming that where life was in danger and people acted threateningly, then the military had the right to shoot if necessary. If one of the rioters was killed by accident, then the army could not be held responsible. There had only been a small number of police present and they could not be expected to defend themselves in the face of such adversity. The military had to interfere and it was for the jury to listen to the military and the police. One soldier had been seriously injured and taken to Chester. His evidence was vital but it was not known whether he would be well enough to attend. The coroner went on to say that he himself had been in King Street whilst the firing had occurred. He had been advised to retire to his home for his own safety, and had seen nothing of the riot.

The coroner, having had his say, decided that the inquest be adjourned until the morning, when it would resume in the County Hall. The 'independent' jury was therefore dismissed for the night, but with the coroner's instruction still ringing in the members' ears that the army could not under any circumstances be held responsible for the deaths.

Not a scrap of evidence had been submitted to the inquest and yet the outcome was more or less cut and dried.

When the proceedings resumed in the morning, several magistrates were in attendance including Trevor-Roper and Henry Potts. Chief Constable Browne was also present. The first to take the stand was Police Inspector Hughes. He related how he and thirty-eight other officers had charge over Ismael Jones and John Jones, with an army escort, to walk to the railway station. The inspector's head was still bandaged from the injuries he received in the riot. He related how the stoning had begun as soon as they reached the gates leading from the Hall Fields onto Chester Street. He himself had maintained hold of the prisoners all the way to the railway station, and on to the platform. Having been heavily struck by a rock, he then handed the prisoners over to Sergeant Lockwood of Overton. The inspector estimated that he had personally been struck between two and three dozen times by rocks and stones.

The coroner intervened at this point and again directed that the army acted lawfully and in self-defence. He regretted the death of Margaret Younghusband who had happened to be in the wrong place at the wrong time.

John William Linnet, a reporter, came to the stand. He said that the noise had attracted him from the Boar's Head, and that he had gone to investigate. He had seen the police and soldiers moving from the Hall Fields to the railway station area with an angry crowd of between two and three thousand in pursuit. At the station, he had seen Captain Blake hold back from giving the order to fire, and also seen him being struck by a rock. He said that hundreds had been throwing stones at the escort, and he had seen the soldiers firing over the heads of the people. He wondered why they had waited so long before firing. He went on to say that he saw a man falling in Tyddyn Street, having been shot by a soldier in the telegraph office at the station. The firing had continued until the train left the station, when it ceased. The crowd's behaviour had stunned him.

Several others took the stand and gave evidence in support of the army. They claimed that the main offenders were the stone throwers, some of whom had been shot dead. Medical evidence was given by doctors who had attended the dead, describing the extent of their injuries and how they had died. The Coroner was moved to ask for further evidence of injuries but the jury members felt that they had heard enough and were more than satisfied. The Coroner on hearing their remarks was in full agreement and asked the jury to retire to deliberate their verdict.

They were out only a short time before they returned to give a verdict of 'Justifiable Homicide' and that they had decided that the army had no alternative than to open fire on the rioters. The foreman said that it had been an unwarranted attack on Her Majesty's Troops and that the deaths of the people involved had been quite justified. Whilst this is true to a certain extent, innocent blood was spilt and at least one innocent life was taken. Whether the bullets were badly or indiscriminately aimed or whether there were ricochets is not known, and no one was called to answer that vexing question.

The failure to read the Riot Act should also have been discussed, regardless of its impracticality. The magistrate who gave the Commanding Officer, Captain Blake, the authority to open fire should still have signed the Act. Mr Clough was only a passenger on the train and nothing more is known about him other than that he claimed to be a magistrate and as such gave the order. He couldn't have signed the necessary paper and therefore, from a legal point of view, the relevant Act was not implemented correctly on the night of the riot. It would have been easy for the authorities to claim that it was impossible to follow the letter of the law under the circumstances, but they never had to defend themselves on this point at any time.

None of the victims were represented at the inquest, which is strange since the death of Margaret Younghusband was contentious to say the very least. But lawyers had to be paid, which may explain why the young woman's death was never fully investigated. The inquest brushed over it with a plea of regret. She was only an orphan girl after all, and what's more had only that morning found a position as the domestic servant of the minister of Capel Mawr in New Street. Her last resting-place was probably at Mold Parish Church graveyard, because anybody of any denomination could be buried there on payment of a fee. As was often the case in those days, unimportant people would not have deserved a permanent marker to record their passing. The curate at the time, one E D James, even failed to record her name correctly in the Parish Records since she appears there as Margaret Young.

THE REPURCUSSIONS

The rioters themselves lay low following the riot since the police were making extensive enquiries and hoped to make arrests in the matter. The first to be arrested was one William Griffiths, a collier of Wrexham Street, Mold who was brought before Mr Trevor-Roper and Mr Henry Potts at 2.00pm on Friday June 5, 1869.

Police Superintendent Bolton gave evidence that he had been on duty and had seen Griffiths throw stones on the day. Griffiths denied the charge making loud claims to the court of 'God Forbid'. The local bandmaster, Mr John Jones, gave evidence that he knew the defendant well and had seen him in the crowd and seen him throwing stones. Griffiths again cried out 'God Forbid'. The case against him pressed ahead and his protestations quieted when the prosecution commented upon the time that Griffiths had been forced to leave the country some twenty years previously. The magistrates adjourned the case until the following Monday and refused the defendant's application for bail.

Elizabeth Jones had died at 11.00pm on the night of June 4 and the inquest into her death was called for the Saturday. It was held at the Boar's Head in Chester Street. Her body was again viewed by the jury and the coroner began to take evidence. Inspector Hughes repeated his evidence from the first inquest. J P Kennain of the Crown Vaults, who was a juror in the original inquest, gave evidence that he had seen the soldiers emerging from the barracks in a rank of four deep to act as an escort to the railway station. The stone throwing began when they reached the gates of the Hall Fields with both men and women being guilty of the throwing. Kennain told the jury that he had seen a woman similar to the deceased throwing stones, and that she had been running up and down the station approach. Having viewed the body, he was now certain that it was the same woman.

A local businessman, Mr Samuel Beresford, said that he saw the deceased being shot by a soldier in the telegraph office, and that she had been throwing stones. He told the jury that he had an excellent view from the railway bridge. The surgeon Mr Trubshaw had seen nothing of the rioting but he had attended Elizabeth Jones until she died. The coroner again said that the army was blameless before dismissing the jury, who returned to give the expected verdict of 'Justifiable Homicide'. They expressed their sympathy to the police and soldiers who had been present on the day, and the inquest was raised.

The police continued in their quest for the worst perpetrators of violence in the riot. William Griffiths was already in custody and he was joined by Abel Tattum of New Street, Mold who was also a member of the Flintshire Militia. Isaac Jones, the husband of Elizabeth Jones, was also arrested and detained. When the police arrested him, they found him grieving over the body of his wife. Isaac Jones was allowed bail to bury his wife but the others were remanded in custody until June 11. Later that summer, ten rioters faced trial in front of Lord Justice Bovill for charges of rioting and assault. Their defence was paid for through collections amongst colliers and their families.

Only one of the ten, Richard Jones, was found not guilty and the others received ten years each. Reports say that the crowd hissed and booed in court, but there was no further rioting and no attempts to release the prisoners this time.

John Young returned to Leeswood Green Colliery shortly after the riot, and all the colliers walked out in disgust refusing to return while he was on site. He was however a very persistent man and tried again to take up his position on June 22. This time he was abducted, taken to Queensferry Station and sent right out of the county. David Phillips of Coed-talon, who worked at the Cae Blyddyn Colliery and who persuaded Ismael Jones to surrender to the police following his release from custody by the crowd on the day of the original trouble, appeared before the court on August 8, 1869, charged with assaulting Young who claimed he was a ringleader.

Throughout his trial, Philip insisted that he had always advocated that violence should not be used. He also claimed that he had offered Young a drink of lemonade throughout the journey from the colliery to the railway since the day was so hot. He said that he had offered every comfort to Young on the journey, but that it was for the best that Young left the area. The prosecution concentrated on his past as a bare-knuckle prize-fighter, which he did not deny but said that he had given it all up since he accepted religion.

The court was not impressed and gave him eighteen months in gaol with hard labour. It is not at all clear what his crime had been for there was no evidence whatsoever that he had done anything wrong. And surely a man couldn't go down for eighteen months just because he had spent time fighting for money. Robert Jones received three months with hard labour for assaulting Young and nineteen-year-old Thomas Gibbons received fourteen days, also with hard labour. The area remained quiet after this latest court appearance, but John Young finally accepted that his position in the area was untenable. His destination was not recorded. David Phillips opened a greengrocer's shop in Coed-talon upon his release from prison.

THE MAGISTRATES

The riot resulted from a number of factors, as becomes apparent from studying this case. Without doubt though, the largest contribution to inflaming the crowd to fever pitch on the day of the trial was the insensitivity of the magistrates and their refusal to accept any evidence in support of the Welsh colliers. The mine owners had decided to cut wages at a time when the handful of English colliers at Leeswood Green were blatantly earning far in excess of their Welsh colleagues. The bench also chose to ignore the fact that Young had no sign whatsoever of physical injury despite the punishment he was alleged to have received at the hands of the colliers. So who were these men who sat in judgement on the colliers and what part did they play in the social structure of the area over which they presided.

Charles James Trevor-Roper was the chairman of the bench and was appointed Magistrate in 1851. He lived at Plas Teg Hall and was a landowner in the area. Plas Teg is now open to the public and stands on the A541, the road from Mold to Wrexham. The Trevor-Roper family had considerable mining and iron making interests in Staffordshire but it is unclear what mining interests they had locally at the time of the riot. Records do exist however of collieries on the Plas Teg estate from the 17th century.

Thomas Wynn-Eyton was appointed Magistrate in 1869 only a few months before the riot occurred. The family home was Leeswood Hall, still a private residence known locally as The White Gates because of the huge gates erected by Sir George Wynne-Eyton. The family had a chequered history but by the time of Thomas Wynne-Eyton the fortunes were smiling upon them again. The exact nature of Wynne-Eyton's investments is not recorded but he was a wealthy man with local mining interests in the Leeswood / Coed-talon area. He was commissioned as an officer of the Flintshire Yeomanry from January 31, 1831 until May 31, 1838, this being a direct forerunner of the Flintshire Constabulary. What is astounding however is that he was the principal owner of the Leeswood Green Colliery at the very centre of all the trouble.

Charles Butler Clough was appointed Magistrate in 1850. He was the vicar of Mold until he was appointed Dean of St Asaph. There are no records that he had mining interests in the area. Henry Potts was appointed Magistrate in 1854. He lived in Glanrafon Hall in Loggerheads near Mold. He was a landowner and his family gave its name to a highly respected firm of solicitors in the area. It is unknown whether he had any mining interests in the area. Colonel Wills was appointed Magistrate in

1847. He lived at Plas Billin, Northop and was a gentleman landowner and farmer. The extent of his mining interests are not known, or whether he had any, although there were several small collieries in the vicinity of his home.

Edward Pemberton was appointed Magistrate in 1839. He lived at Rhos Isa Bistre near Buckley. He was a country landowner and farmer but it is not known whether he had any mining interests in the area. What is known is that he, like Wynn-Eyton, was commissioned an officer of the Flintshire Yeomanry on January 31, 1831 and remained so until June 26, 1832. The date of the Reverend Jenkins-Davies's appointment as Magistrate is not known and neither is it known whether he had any mining interests.

Magistrates under the current rules cannot sit on a bench to hear a case where they have interests. For example a major land-owning magistrate cannot sit on a case where someone is charged with poaching pheasants if the magistrate himself keeps pheasants. The same is true of a shop-owning magistrate being unable to sit in judgement over a shoplifting case. Bias could not be blamed on an individual magistrate in such cases and the current rules make total sense.

Two of the most prominent magistrates sitting on the original Leeswood Green case were Trevor-Roper and Wynne-Eyton. Not only is there a whiff of bias here, the former owned coalmines in Staffordshire and the latter not only had local mining interests, he was actually the owner of the colliery at the centre of the whole trouble. John Young was Wynne-Eyton's representative at the colliery, and here he was sitting in judgement over a group of men who did not exactly see eye to eye with his own representative. What is more, he and Pemberton had been commissioned officers of the forerunner of the Flintshire Constabulary, which again leaves a bad taste in one's mouth regarding either of the two's impartiality in a case such as this.

The case was concluded at an alarming rate, the magistrates coming to a decision without hearing a vast body of evidence. There were over three hundred colliers at Leeswood Green on the morning of June 25, 1869 but only four were called forward to give evidence. The fact that all their evidence was overwhelmingly in support of the defendants might go a long way to explaining why no more were allowed to appear as witnesses. It all gives a very strong impression that the colliers had no hope, and that the magistrates had the case cut and dried regardless of any evidence that came before the bench. Justice was not in contention at this case.

NATIONAL OUTRAGE

The London press had a field-day slating the colliers for the hostilities in the Flintshire and Denbighshire coalfield. The London Illustrated News offered copious coverage, the blame being laid fairly and squarely with the colliers whilst they supported the owners without question. The army was exonerated of any suggestion of blame in the matter. All the press demanded more attention from the police and militia in such riots. There were however some muted attempts to suggest that conditions for the colliers of north Wales were not what they might have been, and that some owners were not looking after their men. But the papers' greatest concern was the riot – it was great news because it was so shocking. The reasons for the riot were only briefly described and analysed, and the part of the magistrates in the original court case was not deemed important enough to be discussed at all. The radical Welsh language paper *Y Faner ac Amserau Cymru* carried the riot story as did all the papers of the day, and its angle on the story might give some indication of the sanctimonious holier than thou attitude that was prevalent at the time. The end of the piece, here translated in full, suggests however that there might be more to this story than met the eye.

The bloody affray that occurred in Mold last week could do little less than cause severe concern in anyone who feels any pride in our national character. This is how the matter came about. Some time ago, warning was given that the colliers wages would be reduced. Whether the owners had sufficient reason, we know not. However, the colliers decided to stay out, and had as much right to do so as the owners had to reduce wages. Had they acted in a gentlemanly and peaceful way, they might well have achieved their ends. But rather than opposing their bosses through legal means, they adopted illegal and violent methods that caused a grave result. They seem to have gathered that Mr Young, the work's supervisor, was the cause of the reduction (in wages) and attacked his house. They made him dirty and carried his furniture to the railway station.

Writs were raised as a result of this illegal act against eight men said to be part of the affray. One man, William Hughes, was caught but a crowd of colliers released him as he was led through the streets. Only four policemen were in charge of him, and they jumped at their chance. Had he received sterner attention, maybe the tragedy could have been avoided. Having taken him a short distance however, they then returned him. When the case came before magistrates, he was released on bail.

On Wednesday, this man and another came before the local magistrates who sent them to goal for a month. Having experienced the dangerous elements that had arisen in the town and area – for no less than a thousand people took part in the first affray – it was expected that the magistrates would not court providence by ordering that the prisoners be walked through streets filled with people armed with stone and staff. But incredibly, the order was given and another attack was made in an attempt to release the prisoners. The way the policemen suffered the attack was a credit to their patience, bravery and resolution. But the crowd became so incensed that it was necessary to send for reinforcements from the 4th Regiment at Chester. The soldiers had plenty to do on arriving, and the crowd refused to disperse no matter what the authorities did. Storms of stones were thrown at the soldiers and police; at last the order to fire was given. The first volley went skywards, in the hope that the crowd would heed the warning. They were however even more incensed and the next volley was aimed at the worst offenders. Three suffered fatal wounds and many others were badly injured. The wife of Isaac Jones, who is in custody, has since died of her wounds. The crowd then dispersed of course, and attempts at causing further affray ceased. The soldiers returned to Chester with clear signs on tunics and faces that they had faced a hard fight. Many believed that, without rucksacks to protect them, many would have died. The injured soldiers and policemen are all expected to recover fully.

If the reduction of wages is proven wrong, even that will fail to exonerate the workers. They should employ more seemly, civilised and Christian methods of standing up for their rights. Although we have the utmost sympathy with the working classes, and have defended their rights at all opportunities and will do so again, we must on this occasion express our opinion that the course of action taken at Mold was a grave mistake. They can be sure that they will do no good to themselves through such actions, and that they are certain to spoil their character and their situation, and many have surely realised their madness. Peaceful and moral means are most effective in ending all troubles. Violence only makes things worse: and the result almost invariably goes against the perpetrators.

The soldiers firing into the crowd without doubt causes concern; but according to all sources of information open to us, their only other choice was to die, thus allowing the terrorists to have their way. Had this been their course of action, they would be failing their country. The jurors at the inquest felt that it was their duty to state that the soldiers, in the circumstances, did nothing more than was expected of them. We are in no doubt that the whole country will agree with their verdict.

Because the official enquiry into the above is not yet over, it would be inappropriate to make further comment, other than noting the main facts that appear to have occurred.

RIOTOUS FLINTSHIRE AND DENBIGHSHIRE

The riot of 1869 was the first in which people were killed by the army in Mold and the surrounding area, although people had been killed in riots in other areas of the United Kingdom. Rioting in itself was certainly not a new occurrence in the coalmines of Flintshire and Denbighshire, and there were numerous reasons for this.

The population of the area increased greatly during the 1790s and the local landowners, who employed most of the people in various capacities, had started to fence off land to prevent the people from grazing animals or growing crops on what had, until then, been regarded as common land. People as a result starved and Thomas Jones, a Leeswood man, pulled down an amount of fencing. He was sent to Fflint Castle for his troubles. Men from Kinnerton, Penyffordd and Brymbo met at the Bridge Inn in Pontblyddyn where the landlord gave them a half-pint of beer. They then set off for Fflint gaol where they attacked the premises, broke windows and put the fear of God into all the staff. Two men were eventually allowed into the building and Jones was freed. The men returned to Pontblyddyn for some more ale. On the way home through Penyffordd and Hertsheath, they pulled up all the fencing they could find en-route. Other colliers joined them at Hope and three Justices of the Peace were called to read them the Riot Act but to no avail since records show that the colliers were '...engaged in great riot'.

Sir Roger Mostyn, the pre-eminent landowner in the area, called for the '...stiffest of punishment to be delivered to the colliers'. A number of Warwickshire Militia were soon brought in to protect the homes of nobility, landowners and Justices of the Peace. A number of the rioters came up before the next Assize Court but the judges decided that the best course of action would be to free the accused for fear of further rioting. The result was that all those involved in the affair were pardoned.

This caused considerable consternation amongst the local bigwigs who felt that the common people were running the sway. They therefore began to employ their own selected men to form a private Militia that would protect them. One hundred men received £10 per annum to be members of the Denbighshire Militia.

By 1795 there was famine throughout the area of Flintshire and Denbighshire. Large gangs of colliers roamed the two counties armed with cudgels and staves looking for food. Rising prices, fuel shortages and black marketeers all added to the unrest. The Navy and Militia Act was passed in an attempt to redress the matter and in answer to the gentry's demands. The act allowed magistrates to select men for service in the Navy or in the local militia. The Act led to further unrest and Justices of the Peace were taken hostage at a public house in Denbigh, where they were forced to sign a paper to the effect that they would not implement the Act within the area.

Flintshire raised three hundred men for the County Militia because the regular soldiers were by now involved in the war with France. The three hundred were soon stretched to the very limits as crowds broke into warehouses in Mold and stole food, including grain and cheese. The landowners called in the militia in scenes that must have been similar to those seen in France a decade earlier when starving people were instrumental in causing the downfall of the old order.

The local gentry decided that what was needed was a stronger force and so funded the forming of the Flintshire Yeomanry Cavalry. The hard winter of 1799/1800 brought further trouble as grain supplies failed again and there were serious riots in Mold, Wrexham and in Holywell. During 1800, matters got so out of hand that the 'Bow Street Runners' were called in to Mold to maintain the peace. Many of the large farms were attacked and some were even set alight.

Working conditions and the working man's sense of general unfairness eventually came to replace starvation as the main reason for rioting. During the early 19th century, people began to stand up for their own rights. The rampant and blatant profiteering of the mine owners was causing consternation among the working class. People came to realise that the cake was being cut very unfairly, with the largest portion by far going into the pocket of the owners. Owners and management invariably set working conditions to maximise the profitability of the concern in the short term. The workers' safety and well being were very much secondary considerations, if they were considered at all by the vast majority of employers. Matters did improve slowly as the political infrastructure of the country matured, but changes more often than not occurred as a result of workers demonstrating rather than as a result of far-sightedness on the part of the leaders. To be fair, there were also instances where workers opposed improvements if it would mean an adverse effect on their pockets in the short term. And the amount that the men, and women and children, took home at the end of the week was more often than not the cause of most of the trouble. The owners considered it far cheaper to protect themselves than to pay their workers a fair wage for their work.

By 1825 the Flintshire Yeomanry Cavalry had formed a garrison in Mold where they maintained a strong presence. They were often called upon to maintain order. In 1826 rioting occurred at the Bromfield

Colliery near Mold when the management tried to change to an eight-hour shift system as had been done in the Cornish tin-mines. The men were not happy but the managers refused to relent and serious rioting occurred. The army moved in but had great difficulty in containing the troubles. It spread throughout the county and resulted in extra troops being called in from the Royal Maelor Cavalry in Wrexham. The situation in Mold at this time was described as '...the most serious of rioting we have had...' The cavalry patrolled the town for twelve days and records state that '...there was much blood shed...'

The cavalry was ever present in Coed-talon from 1825 to 1827 because of the prevalence of serious unrest in the collieries there. Serious rioting occurred in Denbigh in 1828 when public houses and farms were burnt to the ground. In 1850, when two Cornishmen came looking for work in Holywell, the local colliers withdrew their labour and colliers from Halkyn moved in to support their colleagues in their fight. In 1852 there was further serious unrest in the area between Prestatyn and Hollywell where troops were again engaged. The trouble was over English labour being employed at the pits. In 1856, colliers from Wrexham met at Rhosllannerchrugog to protest against the new working conditions. They attacked the local British Iron Company at Acrefair, which was a frequent target for hostilities, and one hundred and forty troops were called from Wrexham to quell the riot.

Six hundred men downed tools in Coed-talon in 1863 after six Welshmen were sacked and replaced by six colliers from Lancashire. The strike was a bitter one, and some two thousand colliers and their wives marched to the manager's house to demand reinstatement of the sacked men. The manager would not listen and the women attacked him violently. During the ensuing upset, an unknown party fired shots and the manager was wounded. The crowd proceeded to wreck his house as well as others in the locality. The Lancashire colliers were then rounded up along with the manager and taken to Mold railway station. Somewhere in Chester Street the manager managed to escape and hide in a barrel of flour. He was later discovered and placed on the train with a warning to never return. Sixteen men were charged with assault but they were acquitted at the trial.

In 1864, a manager from Holywell was forcibly removed to Mostyn, from where he was sent packing by train. The newly formed Flintshire Constabulary was there to try and contain the situation, but the police were fully stretched to do so. In 1865 there were terrible arson attacks by colliers in Denbigh, with many of the rioters being from outside the area. In the same year there were further riots in Holywell and strike-breakers were taken to Mostyn docks to be sent away by ship. But a large police presence met them on the dockside. Houses were attacked and other property was damaged. The police later raided the homes of the riot leaders in the dead of night. Records state that several officers were armed with cutlasses. The rioters were taken into custody and appeared before the Magistrates Court on June 11, 1865. It was not until April 1867 that they appeared before the Assizes court.

One of the colliers' greatest grievances was the activities of *Tommy* or *Truck* shops in the villages and towns near the collieries. The colliery companies owned them and workers' wives could obtain credit at the shops by producing a 'chit' which was given in-lieu of wages. There are reports of women fainting from hunger and fatigue whilst waiting in the queue outside these shops, especially in cold weather. The reason for this was that the normal practise was to allot certain days to certain workers. For instance, a Tuesday might be the day for colliers' wives; Wednesdays might be for coal-cutters, Thursdays for the engineering staff and so on. Nothing could be obtained if a household ran out before the next allotted day, and many people suffered greatly. No other shops offered credit so they were tied to the one Tommy shop, which invariably charged the top prices. The goods they sold were often of a very poor standard, and to balance the odds even further in the owners' direction, serving short measures was prevalent at many shops. On the other hand, many families ran up a large credit at such shops and then did the famous 'moonlight flit' when they couldn't pay the bill.

One notorious shop almost caused a potentially violent battle on Gutter Hill at Rhosllannerchrugog on December 28, 1830. Four thousand colliers and their wives accompanied by quarrymen, rose to complain about the conditions, and in particular a rogue Tommy shop, in Sir Watkin Williams-Wynn's collieries. The Riot Act was read and the colliers demanded that it be read in Welsh. The main culprit here however was a shop in Acrefair. To Sir Watkin's credit, he took heed of the colliers' complaints and agreed to look into the matter. The shop was closed and the manager of the area, a Mr Woods, was sacked. It is said that he had to subsequently seek refuge in a cottage on the main street in Ruabon, near the Wynnstay Public House and that, after dark, he escaped by borrowing some ladies clothing and then swimming across the Dee to safety.

Another great problem, and far more lethal than a Tommy shop, was that of firedamp. This is caused by methane gas which, when mixed with a certain quantity of air, can become highly combustible in a matter of seconds. In 1828, eleven men died at a Holywell colliery when a ball of fire that moved quicker than a fit man could run swept through the face and engulfed everyone. Another serious problem was water, as was witnessed in 1837 when Afon Alun broke through the face at the Argoed Colliery in Mold and flooded the pit before the colliers had a chance to escape. Among the dead were the father and the brother of the novelist Daniel Owen (see Appendix 3). Death came unexpectedly and from many different sources underground. In 1849 an eleven year old boy called Oliver Bagshaw was pulling a pyche underground in Holywell when a brick fell from the roof of the pit. It fell on to his head and killed him on the spot.

The colliers' greatest problem was that they were not united in their complaints. This problem was not confined to the colliers, for the same could be said of workers in the other major heavy industry in north Wales, especially the quarrymen of the west who worked in great adversity and were treated like slaves by the quarry owners and managers, who were again English in many cases.

On a cold blustery night, soon after the Mold Riot, on the coast at Bagillt in a pub called the Boot Inn, a number of colliers met after closing hours to discuss forming 'The Flintshire and Denbighshire Miners Friendly Association'. A precedent had been set in the Lancashire coalmines and these associations went on to become the forerunners of the Union of Miners. The aim was to have a united front when they needed to consult the owners and to ask for better working conditions above and especially below ground. Another of their intentions was to stabilise their wages. The owners hardly welcomed the new Association. After all, they had the military and the courts in their pockets.

CONCLUSION

The story of this important piece of Welsh history was on the lips of the people of Mold until recently. It was a part of our memory, and much more so than the names of the kings and queens of England, or what bits of the globe were coloured pink to show that they were, for a short time, a part of the British Empire. Studying history is a strange phenomenon. The facts that were shoved down our throats in school history lessons were far away and unimportant in our greater scheme of things, but the story of the Mold Riot was right there on our doorstep, and what's more we heard it from our parents and grandparents. We could leave our houses and walk the same streets as the rioters walked on that evening in June 1869. There had been vast changes of course, but the street names were the same and this was where it had all happened.

Mold has changed even more in the past two or three decades – it has grown enormously and the whole structure of the town is different. The teaching of history has also changed, in many respects for the better since pupils are now taught to think about history rather than rely on being force-fed fact after fact and date after date. But the thing that has changed Mold the most is time. Events from so long ago are hardly important to the busy people as they go about their daily toil.

But these events did not end at rocking the social foundations of what was then a small, but certainly not sleepy, market town. The whole of Britain and further afield felt the changes that were caused by the Riot. Far-reaching decisions were made regarding the policing of the country, and politicians and authorities were forced into thinking out a strategy for controlling large-scale civil disobedience. The colliers were also forced into thinking out a more united front to help them vent their grievances to the owners.

APPENDIX 1

PC Jones's daybook recording his life as a policeman in Pontblyddyn is now retained at Hawarden County Record Office. It is a beautifully written, fascinating book giving a day to day and hour by hour account of the officer's duties in the tiny village. Chief Constable Browne's name often appears in the book since he was a frequent visitor due to the constant problems at the local collieries. It seems that there were three officers at this small village, and they often worked fourteen or more hours a day. The daybook records how Jones would get to Mold to start his duty at 8.00am on Fair Days, working through until midnight and then returning to Pontblyddyn to sleep until he returned to hoofing the village beat early the next day.

Colliers were mostly arrested for being drunk or for related offences. This strikes an odd chord since most of the almost daily riots were related to low pay and poor conditions. And yet, being drunk was almost the order of the day. Jones records that the fine for drunkenness was 2/6d. The tale is told of Richard Williams, a collier who stole one hundredweight (about 50Kg) of manure, and was brought before the Revd Jenkins-Davies who remanded him in custody for two days. This was presumably the end of his punishment, and is in itself very severe considering that all he had taken was a few days' waste product from a well-fed cow.

The officer visited the collieries daily in search of tramps who were particularly keen on sleeping rough at the Leeswood Green Colliery and Gas Plant. When he found any, he cautioned them and sent them packing from the area. A record from March 1, 1868 has him cautioning a William Johnson for allowing his donkey to stray on the highway. He arrested Ismael Roberts of Leeswood for stealing three hens, for which he received fourteen days with hard labour from the magistrates' court. Another often found summons in the daybook is to the local alehouses for selling poor quality ale. Riding horses without reins, apart from being downright dangerous, was considered a terrible offence.

One of the local devils who made frequent appearances in the pages was Joseph Williams of Leeswood. His heinous crimes included allowing his donkey to stray on the highway, and leaving his cart unattended on the roadway. It does not record whether the donkey was attached or not, but this was obviously one dangerous criminal.

An important weekly task was to visit the small stream that runs from where the Leeswood Cannel Company to join Afon Alun near where the Pontblyddyn Cricket Ground is now situated. He was detailed to check for pollution from the coal gas extraction plant, which could include oil getting into the river. The same stream causes problems today, but because of sewage discharges. The officers of the Environment Agency now police it.

The only record of his meeting John Young and the three hundred colliers at Hope Junction is to give the time that he and his fellow officer were at the station. References to the rioting in Mold are confined to an entry of 'On duty in Mold' on four consecutive days.

The entries are dominated though by two factors, these being the service of Bastardy summonses in the area and the ever open eye on the collieries that remained volatile during the whole period that they were open in Coed-talon and Leeswood. It gives a wonderful insight into the life of a small village police station in the 19th century, when there was little time for an officer to idle about, and when the distance they walked daily was considerable.

APPENDIX 2

In 1869, the Kings Own (4th) Regiment was based at Chester Castle, which has been the home of the Cheshire Regiment since 1873. The regiment, and the British Army, had gained considerable experience of civil unrest in India. There was not a civilian force there to keep the peace; therefore all such duties were in the hands of the army. One important lesson learnt in India was that opening fire over the head of a rioting crowd was useless, and indeed far more likely to incite the rioters on to even greater deeds. They had also found on the subcontinent that firing into a crowd incensed them even more and that it more often than not resulted in the infliction of even greater damage on the populace, and woe betide any soldier that the rioting crowd managed to get its hands on. What was more, any subsequent rioting was more likely to be better planned, and the crowd was more likely to start the whole affair at a higher fever pitch. The soldiers were only equipped with single shot rifles and stood little chance in the face of a large, determined and maddened crowd.

The men at Mold were experienced in dealing with riots, which might explain the reluctance to open fire. They also knew that Flintshire had its own regular constabulary and felt that it was their duty to maintain law and order. Captain William Francis Blake had joined the regiment in 1857 as an Ensign and was promoted to Lieutenant in 1858. He was promoted to Captain shortly before the events in Mold in 1869 and went on to be promoted to brevet Major and then brevet Lieutenant Colonel in 1881. He died on July 1, 1881 in Barbados whilst serving in the West Indies.

Following the Mold Riot, meetings were held between the military and politicians where the army urged that police forces, where they existed, took charge and received the correct training to cope with major rioting. After all, they wouldn't be short of practise. The military authorities held that their men were not trained for dealing with civil disobedience and encouraged the political authorities to form constabularies where none previously existed. This was the period when unarmed police forces came into being across the land, leaving the army free to concentrate on the matters for which they were trained so that they needn't ever again listen to the Riot Act.

This long legal document was one of the most boring tracts of language that was ever cobbled together to be read out to a bunch of irate citizens on the rampage. Maybe the authors intended to bore their audience to death and, if this didn't work, then shoot them. In practise it is doubtful whether many taking part in a riot actually understood any of the legal gobbledy-gook as it was bawled out by the person with the loudest voice in the vicinity of the riot, who was not actually participating in the riot. By the time such a person had been located and managed to get his teeth and tonsils around the intricate linguistic maze, the riot had usually reached its zenith or burnt itself out.

APPENDIX 3

Daniel Owen was a Mold tailor who had a shop on New Street and lived in the Maes-y-dre area of the town. After his father and brother died in the Argoed Colliery disaster, he was brought up by his mother. There was no such thing as welfare in those days, and single mothers had a very tough time of it. She took in washing to survive and the family lived in conditions of the severest poverty. His mother secured Daniel a position as an apprentice tailor with Angell Jones in New Street when he was twelve. Some years later he spent some time in the Methodist college in Bala with his sight on becoming a preacher, but returned after two and a half years to his tailoring. He worked again for Angell Jones for a time and then started his own venture with a partner.

He received very little education in early life but was an avid reader and spent his working time with tailors who all read to pass the day at their toil. He was encouraged to write and produced sermons for himself and for others in the area. Indeed, his first published original work was a collection of his sermons as well as five stories entitled *Offrymau Neillduaeth a Cymeriadau Methodistaidd* in 1879. His first true novel was *Rhys Lewis*, first published in monthly instalments in the Methodist periodical *Y Drysorfa* between 1882 and 1884. It is a tale that turns around the discussions of the *Seiat* at a chapel very much like Capel Mawr in New Street, where Owen was a regular. The backdrop to the whole story is the Mold Riot, a point that he himself always denied. It has an abusive underground manager in a man called Mr Strangles. Daniel Owen refused to accept that he was based on John Young, but the people of Mold always knew better. *Rhys Lewis* has been called the first great Welsh novel and he went on to complete two more novels, *Enoch Huws* (1891) and *Gwen Thomas* (1894). His work does not translate into English and great writer as he undoubtedly was, he never really grasped the ability to form the perfectly structured novel.

Daniel Owen was always portrayed as the archetypal Methodist, non-smoking, non-drinking Victorian. The reality was somewhat different and attempts were invariably made to try to cover-up his womanising and drinking. This was not easy in a small market town like Mold with a population then of only about one thousand. In fact, the term 'mission impossible' comes to mind. Many of the old timers, none of whom have been around for a few decades now, remembered or heard their parents remembering the old man sitting cross-legged on a bench nursing a hang-over whilst he wrote his next sermon or stitched his next suit.

Mold today has a number of attractions dedicated to this colourful

Victorian bachelor who is known as the father of the Welsh novel, and many of his working tools are preserved in the Daniel Owen Centre in the town.